THE BROKEN WINDOW
ONE ACT EDITION

By
Diane Wagner

LICENSING & PRODUCTION INQUIRIES
Uproar Theatrics, LLC.
hello@uproartheatrics.com | www.UproarTheatrics.com

The Broken Window copyright © 2024 by Diane Wagner

The Broken Window is published by Uproar Theatrics, LLC
500 8th Ave FRNT 3, #1714 New York, NY 10018

ISBN: 978-1-968051-29-7

First Printing, May 2025

CHARACTERS

Ronnie	trans or non-binary (AFAB), brooding, 17
Suzanne	athletic, type A personality, 17
Tricia	straightforward, 17
Megan	innocent, insecure, 17
Angie	mainstream, looks slightly more mature than the others, 17
Killian	Suzanne's younger brother, a charismatic stoner, 15
Kevin	Killian's friend, a reluctant observer, 15
Dani	a ghost, 15

TIME
The present, just after midnight.

SETTING
An abandoned house with three sections visible to the audience. On the second story, there is a large bedroom center stage with two windows, one with a broken pane of glass. There is a small hallway outside the door of the bedroom just at the top of a staircase. The front door of the house is downstage right and the dining room is downstage left; both are connected by a foyer. The place is dilapidated since it hasn't been inhabited for about three years. The rooms still have some furniture along with various remnants of having once been lived in. There is no electricity in the house so the stage should appear to be lit by Ronnie's camping lantern, flashlights, and moonlight.

*At rise, Ronnie, wearing a hooded sweatshirt, is
upstairs in the bedroom seated on the floor,
blending in with the furniture. The house is
dimly lit by moonlight. Noises of the night can
be heard from outside. The mood is eerie, lonely
for a few beats, followed by the sound of
floorboards creaking. Someone else is moving
around in the house. Ronnie hears it, removes
his hood, and listens intently.*

*Megan enters DSR with a folded note in one
hand and a flashlight in the other. She shines the
light on the house, debating whether or not to go
in. The wind kicks up, and a dog howls in the
distance, prompting her to open the door and go
inside.*

MEGAN
(*breathless*) Oh God. Oh my God. What am I doing?

*Hearing the door open and close, Ronnie stands
and slowly moves to the door of the bedroom.
Megan hears the floorboards creaking.*

MEGAN
(*shining her flashlight down the hallway*) Hello? Who's
there?

RONNIE
(*after a beat, from the bedroom*) Hello?

MEGAN

Oh God.

RONNIE
(*looking down the stairs*) Megan?

1

Megan shines her flashlight up the stairs, sees Ronnie and screams.

RONNIE

Sshhhhhh! Stop! The neighbors will hear you.

MEGAN

Veronica!?!

RONNIE

Don't scream. Nobody can know we're here.

MEGAN

What is going on?!

Suzanne enters from DSL, also terrified. She shines her flashlight on the house, makes her way to the front door and listens.

RONNIE

Stop shouting, Megan!

MEGAN

I… I got this note.

RONNIE

I know.

MEGAN

Did you get one too?

RONNIE

Just… Please, just come upstairs.

MEGAN

Upstairs? Are you crazy? I'm not going up there!

*Hearing voices from within, Suzanne slowly
opens the door. Megan screams. Which causes
Suzanne to scream. Which causes Ronnie to
drag them both further into the hallway.*

RONNIE

Guys, you have to shut up! The neighbors are gonna hear us.

SUZANNE

What is happening? I came because I got this note. Why are
you here?

MEGAN

Because I got one too. Do you think somebody is trying to
kill us?

RONNIE

No!

SUZANNE

How do you know?

RONNIE

I just… no, that is not what's happening… come upstairs.

SUZANNE

This is the stupidest thing I've ever done.

MEGAN

Me too.

SUZANNE

Stupid. Stupid. Stupid.

RONNIE

If it's so stupid, then why did you come?

SUZANNE

I came because I thought someone might be in trouble.

RONNIE

Well someone IS in trouble.

SUZANNE

What?

MEGAN

Oh no. No, no, no.

The floorboards creak in another part of the house causing all of them to freeze. Tricia enters DSL.

SUZANNE

Is someone else in this house?

Tricia bangs dramatically on the front door causing Megan and Suzanne to scream again. Ronnie pushes past them to open the door and hustle her in.

RONNIE

Get inside.

TRICIA

What is going on?

SUZANNE

Tricia?

TRICIA

Suzanne?

MEGAN

Oh no. I have to pee..

TRICIA

Megan?

MEGAN

Yes. Hello, Tricia. Great. I just peed a little.

A porch light switches on at the neighbors.

RONNIE

Are you kidding me right now?

MEGAN

Guys, you know I hate scary stuff. My bladder can't take it!

RONNIE

We gotta go upstairs.

MEGAN

Not to mention my IBS.

RONNIE

If the neighbors see us here they're gonna call the cops!

SUZANNE

The cops?

MEGAN

OH MY GOD!

RONNIE

(*heading upstairs*) It'll be fine. Just follow me.

5

TRICIA

This is so messed up.

They ascend the staircase and enter the room.

SUZANNE

Do you think there are rats in here?

RONNIE

Maybe. But I haven't seen any yet.

MEGAN

Yet?

SUZANNE

You do know rats carry the plague.

MEGAN

THE PLAGUE!?

They've all entered the bedroom.

RONNIE

Please, calm down. Nobody is getting the plague!

TRICIA

What are you all doing here?

SUZANNE

Uh… the note!

TRICIA

So you got a note too?

SUZANNE

We all got notes.

TRICIA

What does yours say?

SUZANNE

(*reading*) "Urgent. Need help. Go tc the house on Prospect at midnight."

MEGAN

My note says the exact same thing.

TRICIA

Mine too. (*looking at Ronnie*) Is that what yours says, Veronica?

> *They all look at him now. There is an awkward*
> *silence as the rest of them realize he's not*
> *holding a note.*

SUZANNE

Wait. You didn't get one?

MEGAN

So how did you know to come here?

TRICIA

Oh my God, Megan. Really?

MEGAN

What? (*grasping*) Oh! *(to Ronnie) You* wrote the notes?

RONNIE

I did.

TRICIA

I should've known. This has your brand of crazy written all over it.

MEGAN

What is this about?

RONNIE

Well... I'm sorry, but... I really need your help. I just have a lot going on right now... and I was hoping...

SUZANNE

Is this about babysitting?

RONNIE

What? No!

TRICIA

Babysitting?!

SUZANNE

Well, we all know Veronica was obsessed with that babysitting idea. I wouldn't be surprised if this was an elaborate ruse to get the club back together.

TRICIA

The babysitter's club? Are you serious, Suzanne? That lasted about two weeks during 7th grade and between the six of us we only got one job.

MEGAN

For which we were not paid, as I recall.

SUZANNE

That's because my mom was only letting us watch Killian for the experience.

TRICIA

It was an experience alright.

MEGAN

How's Killian doing these days?

TRICIA

Still starting fires?

SUZANNE

He's… in treatment.

MEGAN

Good for him.

Another awkward silence. They look to Ronnie.

RONNIE

I'll explain once everyone is here. And by the way, it's Ronnie.

MEGAN

What? Who?

SUZANNE

Who is Ronnie?

MEGAN

Ronnie is coming here?

RONNIE

No, *I'm* Ronnie. I go by Ronnie now.

MEGAN

Oh! Okay. That's cool. That's great, *Ronnie*. What are your pronouns?

RONNIE

He/Him.

TRICIA

(*under her breath*) Oh God.

RONNIE

I'm sorry, Tricia. Do you have a problem with that?

TRICIA

Uh, no. The *problem* is that we are in an abandoned house in the middle of the night. So trust me, *Ronnie*, your pronouns have very little to do with my discomfort!

SUZANNE

So who are we still waiting for?

TRICIA

Really? Isn't it obvious? Look around and ask yourself who is missing from this group.

Megan and Suzanne gasp.

MEGAN

She's actually going to come here? You really think... I mean, I assume you put the same note in her locker... and you really think... I'm in my jammies here.

TRICIA

Don't worry, Megan. She's not gonna show up.

RONNIE

You don't know that.

TRICIA

She wouldn't be caught dead in this house!

They cringe.

TRICIA

Sorry. I didn't mean -

*Angie enters downstage left, also carrying a
flashlight. She steps into the house without
hesitation.*

MEGAN

I have to agree with you though. I'm sure she took one look
at Ronnie's note and didn't give it a second thought. She
probably crumbled it up and threw it in the nearest -

RONNIE

Shh!

*The girls freeze, terrified by the sound of Angie
ascending the staircase. She enters the room.*

SUZANNE

(*under her breath*) Oh God.

TRICIA

I stand corrected.

RONNIE

Hey, Ang. Thanks for coming.

ANGIE

(*looking around at the group*) What is this? Why are you all
here?

MEGAN

Oh, it's crazy actually. Ronnie put that same mysterious note
in all of our lockers, so we're like just as clueless as you are.
I mean, not that you're clueless, like I'm not saying you're
not smart, I'm just saying… well… we have no idea what

MEGAN (CONT)
we're doing here either and we're all kind of freaking out about it. But yeah. Wow. It's so good to see you, Angie. How are you?

ANGIE
Great.

MEGAN
Cool.

ANGIE
(*to Ronnie*) So what is this?

RONNIE
I know it was a weird thing to do, especially since it's been so long.

MEGAN
Like... almost three years...?

SUZANNE
Weird is an understatement.

TRICIA
It would be a lot less weird if we weren't in an abandoned house.

SUZANNE
This doesn't even feel like the same place..

MEGAN
It's sad, really. You know? I still don't understand why nobody moved in here.

ANGIE
Her parents never sold the house.

SUZANNE

My mom said they never intend to. It's just going to sit here indefinitely… falling apart.

TRICIA

Why did you ask us to come *here*, of all places, Ronnie?

ANGIE

Who is Ronnie?

TRICIA

She is.

MEGAN

HE is.

SUZANNE

Veronica is going by Ronnie now.

MEGAN

And his pronouns are he/him.

Tricia sighs audibly.

RONNIE

Oh my God! What is wrong with you?

SUZANNE

I'm fine with it.

MEGAN

It's great! All good, Ronnie!

ANGIE

I actually don't care.

TRICIA

We're all happy for you, okay? Congratulations, you found yourself. Now will you tell us why you put a note in our lockers to lure us here in the middle of the night? This is very dark, even for you.

ANGIE

I don't even know why I came.

RONNIE

It's just that... It's not easy for me to explain this...

TRICIA

Spit it out!

RONNIE

I'm starting to forget a lot of things. Like very important things. It's like I have this block in my brain. I just... I can't remember.

MEGAN

Like what things?

RONNIE

Simple things like holidays and birthdays, things that I should be able to remember.

MEGAN

That is pretty weird.

RONNIE

And then there are some not so simple things. Like... the night Dani died. I don't remember any of it, and I'm worried about why that is. Like... am I blocking things out because I did something that I don't want to remember?

SUZANNE

Oh my God.

RONNIE

Please, no! I don't mean it like that. Like, you know I wouldn't hurt anybody. I know I didn't... But something is wrong. I called you here because you have the memories! You were there! I know you don't really know me anymore, but you did once. I want to believe you can help me figure this out. Help me fill in the blanks.

ANGIE

You don't need us to fill in the blanks, you need a psychiatrist.

ANGIE goes past RONNIE to leave. He grabs her arm in an attempt to stop her. She breaks free in a panic causing the others to panic too and scramble toward the door.

SUZANNE

I don't like this.

ANGIE

We shouldn't be here.

SUZANNE

(*overlapping/scrambling to leave*) Get me out of here right now!

ANGIE

(*overlapping*) Move! I can barely see in here!

TRICIA

(*overlapping*) Stop pushing!

MEGAN
Guys, stop it! Everybody, calm down! Ronnie, we know you didn't hurt anyone. What happened to Dani was an accident. Can we just pause here for a minute and try to help him?

RONNIE
I know I wasn't there. But for some reason I feel like I was. Like I could see what was happening while it was happening, or like I could hear it.

ANGIE
What are you talking about?

RONNIE
I don't know. I mean, I know, but I don't know how to tell you.

MEGAN
Just try to explain.

RONNIE
I've always had this. Since I was a little kid. Like I hear something in my mind and then someone says it later in the day. Or I get a message -

TRICIA
A message from who?!

RONNIE
I don't know! The universe, angels, spirits!

TRICIA
Oh God.

RONNIE
See this is why I didn't want to tell you.

MEGAN

I get it. It's like intuition.

RONNIE

Yes.

TRICIA

So you're psychic now?

RONNIE

I'm not saying that!

ANGIE

But you hear things?

RONNIE

Yes! *(beat)* I'm hearing something right now.

SUZANNE

What?

RONNIE

It just… it's a voice…

TRICIA

Who's voice?

RONNIE

I hear… or I imagine that I can hear someone calling for help.

MEGAN

Okay. And you're saying this happens to you a lot.

RONNIE

Sometimes. Yes… like after Dani died… I could hear her too.

SUZANNE

I don't want to do this.

TRICIA

You heard Dani calling for help?

RONNIE

No... not calling for help but... I heard her voice.

MEGAN

What did she say?

RONNIE

She said, "it's not your fault."

MEGAN

What? It's not *my* fault?

RONNIE

No, no! Not you, Megan... It was like she was trying to send me some kind of message.

ANGIE starts laughing.

RONNIE

What? You think I'm lying?

ANGIE

I think that you are delusional! See, this is exactly why I don't hang out with any of you anymore. (*starts to leave*) Honestly, you all need to grow up.

TRICIA

Are you serious? You're lumping me into a category with them!

SUZANNE

So rude.

TRICIA is blocking the doorway.

ANGIE

Whatever, Tricia, just move.

TRICIA

No. I am nothing like them and you know it.

ANGIE

Fine. You're not as pathetic as the rest of them.

SUZANNE

Seriously?

TRICIA

But you stopped hanging out with *me* too.

ANGIE

Oh my God! After everything that happened I just needed to go my own way. I shouldn't have to explain that. I'm not doing this. Please move!

RONNIE

Look, I'm sorry I asked you to come here. I should have known this would be triggering.

ANGIE

Triggering? You put a note in our lockers that said HELP, URGENT, DANGER or whatever and asked us to come to our dead friend's abandoned house in the middle of the night. Just being in the same room with all of you is triggering - this is actually insane.

SUZANNE

I agree. What were you thinking, Veronica?

RONNIE and MEGAN

(*correcting her*) Ronnie!

ANGIE

Whatever. What do you actually want from us?

RONNIE

I want your help! I guess I just thought if I asked you to meet *here* you'd actually show up, since our friendship with Dani was the one thing that tied us all together.

There is a painful silence.

RONNIE

You're the only people who really know me. I don't have anyone else…

MEGAN

Ronnie, that can't be true. I mean, we do know a lot about each other's lives. We were always either at your house or here. But I find it hard to believe that you don't have other friends because I see you with people at school. And I… I called you, and you never called me back. I texted. No response. After it happened, I'd look longingly at you in the cafeteria probably for like two months straight, and you'd just look the other way. If you have *no one*, as you say… am I really such a loser that you would choose to be alone over being with me?

RONNIE

No! It's not you, Megan. It's just that when we lost her… I just… I couldn't feel anything… I was shut down. I couldn't be around anyone. Especially any of you. I didn't want to have to think about it. Can't you understand that?

MEGAN

No, I can't. To not even want to speak to any of us. To check
in on us. You never considered how we were feeling…

RONNIE

You don't get it. I didn't want an *US* without her! I didn't
want to exist. I never wanted to be Veronica in the first place,
let alone Veronica without...

TRICIA

We all felt that way!

RONNIE

Oh, you wanted to be someone else, Tricia?

TRICIA

I don't mean that part, but I didn't want to go on without her!
And some of us would have really appreciated having a
friend to turn to in the midst of the worst time in our lives.

SUZANNE

I know I would've.

TRICIA

Is that so? Because you never reached out to me?

SUZANNE

I thought I did…

TRICIA

You most certainly did not, Suzanne.

SUZANNE

Well, it was swim season, and my dad was just kind of over
the top about it -

21

TRICIA

Of course that's your excuse.

MEGAN

I called, I texted... all of you. Every one of you.

SUZANNE

I'm sorry, Megan. Like I said, I was just so busy.

MEGAN

What about the rest of you?

TRICIA

I apologize, Megan. It was rude not to respond. But to be honest, after it happened, I didn't feel the same way about any of you. I'm sorry if that hurts, but I think it's obvious that the only thing that kept us all together for so long was Dani. How much did we really have in common outside of that? Suzanne, I never could relate to you - swimming, gymnastics, cross country - that stuff is your whole life and I couldn't care less about it. Megan, you're sweet, but you've always been sort of immature. Like even in 6th grade you wanted to keep playing with dolls while the rest of us were into boys and makeup.

RONNIE

I wasn't.

TRICIA

No, you were not. And there ya go. One more person I couldn't relate to.

ANGIE

(*laughing*) Wow. That's harsh.

TRICIA

Oh, I'm harsh? (*getting heated*) How about you try to explain why you've had nothing to do with us for the past three years? Why you literally turn the other way when you see us in the halls and act like you don't even know us. You didn't return my calls after it happened. And yes, I actually did call you, Angie, repeatedly, because for some reason, which I cannot fathom now, I actually thought you and I were closer than any of us. Maybe even closer than I was with Dani. I thought you were my best friend, and you ditched me. You might as well have died too!

RONNIE

Oh my God!

MEGAN

It was hard for all of us. We ALL loved her.

ANGIE

True. But to varying degrees.

TRICIA

Right, because you know better than anyone -

ANGIE

Well, let's see... Tricia, you wanted everything she had, including or most especially me as a best friend. Megan, you worshiped her and tried to copy everything she ever did, said, wore - and it was pitiful. Suzanne, you were competitive with her, like dementedly competitive - with grades, sports, popularity, you name it, and Veronica... I'm sorry, Ronnie... You were obviously in love with her, which we all knew and talked about behind your back. But I just loved her - plain and simple. She was *my* friend. My best friend before any of you came along. And losing her was the worst thing that ever happened to me. But after it happened, I found myself strangely relieved to be free of all of you.

23

Shocked silence.

ANGIE
How's that, Tricia? Too harsh?

TRICIA
I'm out. Going back to bed. You all suck.

ANGIE
I'm right behind you.

RONNIE
Please! Don't go. I know it was Dani. I heard her!

SUZANNE
This is crazy!

ANGIE
You're saying that on the night Dani died you heard her voice in your head?

RONNIE
(*struggling*) I don't... Yes, I think so...

ANGIE
Or maybe this is one of those memories you blocked out. Maybe it was you, Ronnie. In her room that night -

RONNIE
No -

MEGAN
We know he wasn't there the night Dani died, so stop suggesting that. Dani was alone in her room and her parents were downstairs.

ANGIE

(*Suddenly realizing*) Oh my God! We're in her room. Why are we in her room?

TRICIA

Ronnie made us come up here!

SUZANNE

I don't want to be here (*crying*)...

RONNIE

It was just instinctive to come up -

ANGIE

You're sick! Why would you ask us to come to this house?

RONNIE

I don't know! I don't even know now what I was thinking!

TRICIA

(*to Ronnie*) You said you thought we'd come if it had something to do with Dani, and you're right! That's the only reason I would do this - I only came because... Forget it.

SUZANNE

No, what?

TRICIA

I don't know... somehow... I can't believe I'm admitting this... I felt like it was...

MEGAN

Like it was Dani?

TRICIA

Yes.

MEGAN

Me too.

SUZANNE

Me too.

TRICIA
Like it was Dani asking for help.

MEGAN

Yes.

SUZANNE

Yes.

They all look at Angie.

ANGIE
Ok, fine. Yes, in some weird way I guess.

MEGAN
What does this even mean?

TRICIA
It means his crazy is rubbing off on the rest of us!

MEGAN
You wrote the note, Ronnie, right?

Killian enters from SR.

RONNIE
Of course I wrote the note.

MEGAN
Oh, okay. Thank God.

RONNIE

But she told me to write it.

> *Killian enters the house and slams the door
> behind him creating a loud bang. Upstairs, they
> all scream, not sure whether to run out the
> bedroom door, hide or defend themselves.*

KILLIAN

Hello?

SUZANNE

(*overlapping*) Who is that?

TRICIA

(*overlapping*) Somebody is in the house!

MEGAN

I knew it!

ANGIE

(*overlapping*) Oh my God.

MEGAN

This was all a plot to kill us.

TRICIA

Shut up, Megan!

MEGAN

We're gonna die!

ANGIE

Just hide!

> *They all try to obscure themselves, except*
> *Ronnie who stands frozen in place, terrified.*

KILLIAN
(*heading up the stairs*) Is someone up there?

ANGIE
Hide, Ronnie!

> *KILLIAN enters the bedroom. Suzanne sees him,*
> *stands up from her hiding place and lets out a*
> *blood curdling scream. Killian screams in terror.*
> *Suzanne hits him repeatedly.*

KILLIAN
Suzanne?

SUZANNE
Killian?

> *She continues hitting him.*

KILLIAN
Owww! Knock it off, you nutbag!

SUZANNE
What are you doing here?

KILLIAN
What are *you* doing here? Don't you need to wake up in an
hour to work out or something?

TRICIA
Wait. This is Killian?

KILLIAN

What is going on?

TRICIA

Wow. You really grew up.

KILLIAN

Yeah, that generally happens to people. (*realizing*) Tricia?

TRICIA

Yeah.

KILLIAN

What up, girl?

ANGIE

Hey, Killian.

KILLIAN

Hey, Angie. Wait... you're with... Seriously, what are you doing here?

RONNIE

Shouldn't we ask you the same thing?

KILLIAN

Well I'm just here to meet a friend

SUZANNE

WHAT??!? In the middle of the night? You are so dead, little boy. I am telling Mom and Dad.

KILLIAN

Go ahead! Nobody cares what I do! And anyway you're here too. So what is actually happening?

SUZANNE

I was summoned here in a most upsetting and inappropriate way, and I am trying to leave. I never should've come.

TRICIA

Same.

ANGIE

Yeah, whatever she said.

KILLIAN

Interesting. Well I just came here to get high, which is what I do pretty much every night. So theoretically, I have more right to be here than the rest of you.

RONNIE

You have no right to be here! This is not your house!

KILLIAN

Oh I'm sorry! Is this your house?

RONNIE

Well... no.

KILLIAN

Bing. Bong. And speaking of... you don't mind if I smoke a little...(*he digs around in his backpack.*)

> *Suzanne, looking inside the backpack, screams again. The others flinch in terror.*

ANGIE

My God, Suzanne! Why did you do that?

SUZANNE

That is drug paraphernalia! My brother is a drug addict!

MEGAN

Okay, I think we should all try to calm down.

KILLIAN

Wait, I know you...

MEGAN

You most certainly do. I was your babysitter, young man.

KILLIAN

This is quite a group you've assembled for a suspicious midnight rendezvous. It's been a pretty long time for you all, am I right?

SUZANNE

Yes.

RONNIE

And it's none of your business.

MEGAN

Wait. Did you say you're meeting someone here, Killian?

KILLIAN

I did say that.

SUZANNE

Who? A drug dealer?!

KILLIAN

Uh, no. I have already made the deal for the drugs. So...

Kevin enters reluctantly through the front door.

KEVIN

Killian? Are you upstairs?

KILLIAN
(*yelling down*) Yeah, bro, it's a party up here.

> *Kevin ascends the staircase and enters the bedroom.*

KEVIN
Oh my God! Suzanne?

SUZANNE
Yes, Kevin. It is me. And I will be telling your mother and mine what I have seen here tonight.

ANGIE
Come on, Suzanne. They're just hanging out.

> *Kevin squeaks.*

KEVIN
(*discreetly to Killian*) Is that Angie Silvonek?

KILLIAN
Yes.

KEVIN
(*crushing, to Angie*) Hey. Hi.

ANGIE
Hello.

> *Awkward silence.*

KILLIAN

Okay... I feel like some decisions need to be made here. It would seem that these girls had a plan to do... something here tonight.... Maybe something weird or witchy... a seance perhaps, and this is conflicting with our plans to get high. So I'm gonna propose that we all just do our own thing. There are plenty of rooms in this house. I'm happy to smoke my dope down in the living room and leave you all to your business, even though I would prefer to remain in this room, 'cuz it's sort of been established as like *my* room.

RONNIE

(*snapping*) This is not your room.

KILLIAN

Woah! Woah, dude! I do not understand your hostility towards me. I have been coming to this place for months and I've never seen you here before. So I think I have dibs.

RONNIE

You have dibs on nothing! You shouldn't even be in this house.

KILLIAN

And you should? Who exactly are you?

SUZANNE

(*discreetly*) That is Veronica, Killian.

KILLIAN

Wait, what?

RONNIE

My name is Ronnie.

> *Killian looks back at Suzanne, then suspiciously back at Ronnie, slowly grasping.*

KILLIAN

Ohhhh. Okay. I know you, dude. It's all good. I assure you,
we mean no harm.

KEVIN

What is going on? I knew I shouldn't have snuck out.

KILLIAN

Kevin, I didn't mention this before, and I probably should
have, but I think it's time I let you in on something. (*drawing
it out for dramatic effect*) You see… years ago… a tragedy
occurred in this house. As legend has it… a young girl died
in this very room.

RONNIE

Oh my God.

TRICIA

Legend has it? It was like three years ago. That's not
legendary, that's recent events. And you were at her funeral,
bozo.

KILLIAN

No need for name calling, dear. I'm just trying to set the tone
here. This is a creepy place, and for some creepy reason, the
five of you, Dani's best friends, have assembled here tonight
in her bedroom. A little curious, am I right?

SUZANNE

Why, God?

KILLIAN

Listen, no pressure. I know these things take time. I'm just
gonna sit back and quietly wait for the seance to commence,
which, by the way, I am all in for.

KEVIN

Please tell me this isn't a seance.

RONNIE

It's not!

KILLIAN

You don't think maybe we should try to summon her spirit to shed a little light on the situation.

KEVIN

What situation? There's a situation?

TRICIA

What is wrong with you, Killian?

SUZANNE

He has significant issues.

KILLIAN encourages KEVIN to sit on the bed.

KILLIAN

You see, Kevin, while the death was deemed "accidental," to this day, there are still a lot of unanswered questions around what really transpired that night.

SUZANNE

Stop it, Killian!

KILLIAN

As I recall, her parents claimed to have been downstairs at the time of her death. It was late at night, ironically, right around this time, and they said they'd fallen asleep while watching TV. When suddenly they were awakened by the sound of breaking glass. So they shot off the couch, scared and confused, then her father shouted, "everything okay up there?" Or something to that effect.

ANGIE

Seriously, Killian, nobody wants to hear this.

KILLIAN

(*caught up in the story*) When Dani didn't answer, her dad got up to investigate. According to his story, just as he reached the bottom of the stairs, he heard a second sound which he described as a thud. Naturally, in retrospect, he and everyone else, upon hearing the story, assumed that thud was the sound of Dani's body hitting the floor.

SUZANNE

Stop!

KILLIAN

But here's where it gets dicey... When Dad entered the room, he noted his daughter's lifeless body which was not on the floor, but *on the bed.*

KEVIN screams and jumps off the bed.

KILLIAN

(*continuing*) Next to her, they found a plastic sandwich baggie containing 2 adderall. Her father let out a blood curdling scream, which was so loud the neighbors heard it. When her mother heard the scream, she rushed up to the room too. This very room! Her parents lost their minds. They wailed and lamented. The mother cradled the body, while the father called 911.

TRICIA

Seriously, shut up!

KILLIAN

(*too carried away*) It was not until the police and paramedics arrived on the scene that someone noticed the broken window in her room. (*Noting one of the windows, which happens to be broken*) HOLY CRAP! That's the actual window! (*eerily*) Still broken after all these years.

KEVIN

(*terrified*) What?!

KILLIAN

When the coroner did an autopsy, he determined the cause of death to be accidental heart failure brought on by the adderall. To this day, no one knows where she got the pills, why she had them or why she decided to take a handful of them on her own, in her bedroom, on a Tuesday night. It was also determined that she had a heart defect that had gone undiagnosed her entire life - so even a lesser amount of amphetamines might have caused her demise. Either way, she took way more than the average dose of adderall which called into question whether or not she intended to take her own life.

RONNIE

THAT IS A LIE!

KILLIAN

No it's not! Everyone was talking about that at the time.

TRICIA

Yeah, everyone who knew nothing about her or the situation.

KEVIN

The whole story is sketchy. Like who ODs on adderall?

SUZANNE

It was an accident!

KILLIAN

That's not even the weirdest part! The coroner also
determined the time of death, as coroners do, to be *hours*
before her parents found her. She went up to her room right
after dinner to study, they said, but they didn't hear the glass
breaking until well after midnight. So here's the big
unanswered question, my friends. If she was already dead,
who broke that window? And furthermore, what on God's
green earth was that thud? And the neighbors, who had been
close with the family for years, reported that she had actually
been fighting with her parents earlier that night. The
shouting at the dinner table was so loud they could hear them
from next door -

RONNIE

SHUT UP! GET OUT OF HERE!

KILLIAN

Woah! I'm just stating the facts.

RONNIE

YOU ARE NOT WELCOME HERE! SHE DOESN'T
WANT YOU HERE!

KILLIAN

Uhhh…. Who doesn't want me here?

MEGAN

Oh no.

TRICIA

Ronnie, please calm down.

RONNIE

SHE IS TELLING ME TO MAKE YOU GO AWAY!

KEVIN

I'm scared!

KILLIAN

Are you saying the dead girl is telling you to give me the boot?

ANGIE

Yes, that's what he's saying.

RONNIE

Please. She just doesn't want you here right now.

KEVIN

So just to clarify, this *is* a seance?

SUZANNE, RONNIE and MEGAN

NO!

TRICIA

No, it is not. We are not here to conjure anyone. So, spirits, if you're listening, stay where you are - do not show yourselves!

SUZANNE

Killian, get out of here! This night has been bad enough, and you're just making everything worse.

KILLIAN

Oh, really? That's not how I see it. You all look like a herd of deer in a pair of headlights. Whereas I am a curious creature of the night. I have actual skills in connecting with the spirit world.

SUZANNE

Not interested.

KILLIAN
(*continuing anyway*) Dani, if you're in here, give us a sign -

TRICIA
(*overlapping*): Shut up, Killian!

KILLIAN
I will not shut up! You got Kevin and I all wrapped up in this now.

SUZANNE
You're not wrapped up in anything. Nothing is happening here!

KILLIAN
A likely story.

RONNIE
Oh no!

MEGAN
It's okay, Ronnie. Let's all get out of here.

RONNIE (*blocking his ears*)
No, no, no, no, no!

TRICIA
Ronnie!

RONNIE
It's happening again.

KEVIN
I'm scared.

KILLIAN
What is happening?

RONNIE

I can hear her! You don't hear that? She's crying!

MEGAN

Who, Dani?

RONNIE

Someone… someone is saying, "Help! Help! Help me!" Oh
my God. (*sobbing*) Oh God! Somebody! Please! HELP ME!

> *The front door of the house opens and closes
> with a slam but no one can be seen entering,
> followed by the sound of floorboards creaking as
> if someone is walking around downstairs.*

KEVIN

What is going on?

TRICIA

Somebody else is in here!

KILLIAN

(*grabbing his backpack*) It's probably the cops.

KEVIN

We're gonna get arrested!

SUZANNE

I hate you, Killian!

KEVIN

Me too!

KILLIAN

Me? How is this my fault?!

ANGIE

Guys, shut up! Everybody, hide!

> *They all scatter around the room attempting to hide behind whatever they can find, except for Ronnie who is frozen in place.*

MEGAN

Ronnie, please! You have to hide.

> *A light illuminates Dani DSR in the foyer. We never see her enter the house, but she can now be seen slowly making her way to the staircase. Though she looks like any other teenage girl, there is something about her appearance that is supernatural. The floorboards creak as Dani walks up the stairs. They all listen intently. The door to the bedroom creaks open and Ronnie clearly sees something the others don't see. Dani appears in the doorway of the bedroom illuminated.*

RONNIE

Dani?

DANI

(*her voice is altered, hollow, distant*) It's not your fault.

> *The lights flash, leaving the kids in darkness for a beat. When they come back on, everyone*
>
> *except for RONNIE and DANI, scream, scatter, and tear down the stairs. TRICIA, SUZANNE, MEGAN, and KEVIN head out the front door, while ANGIE and KILLIAN go into the dining*

room and hide under the table.

Lights up SR on Tricia, Suzanne, Megan and Kevin. They are out of breath standing outside the front door of the house.

TRICIA
(*hysterical*) WHAT WAS THAT?

MEGAN
Oh my God! Oh my God!

TRICIA
This is crazy, right?

MEGAN
Well... Yeah. Obviously.

KEVIN
What do you mean? You don't think Ronnie really saw anything?

TRICIA
Of course he didn't! He's losing his freakin' mind.

SUZANNE is shaking, can't quite catch her breath as if in shock.

MEGAN
(*approaching her*) Suzanne? Are you okay?

She continues to shake, her breathing labored; then she begins to violently sob.

MEGAN
Suzanne, it's okay. Ronnie is just... unwell. He needs help.

KEVIN

What if he's not faking it or imagining it or whatever?

TRICIA

Seeing a ghost?

KEVIN

Yeah.

TRICIA

You actually think Dani's ghost is in that house? Talking to Ronnie?

KEVIN

Maybe...

MEGAN

That is not what's happening.

TRICIA

He's insane! We need to do something!

Suzanne continues to sob violently.

MEGAN

Suzanne, please. You're okay. We're all going to be okay.

TRICIA

Snap out of it, Suzanne. He is obviously lying.

Suzanne looks up at Tricia, trying to catch her breath to speak.

44

SUZANNE

(*through sobs*) I... I just worry that... maybe... that message is for me.

MEGAN

What message, Suzanne?

SUZANNE

(*sobbing*) It's... It's...

MEGAN

It's not your fault.

KEVIN

What's not your fault?

SUZANNE

What happened... to Dani...

TRICIA

Suzanne, Ronnie didn't actually *hear* anything. Ronnie is, in fact, delusional!

SUZANNE

He's not. The message was for me. I know it.

TRICIA

Why are you acting like this? This is -

SUZANNE

Because it was! It was. I know it was.

TRICIA

What was?

SUZANNE

It was all my fault.

*Lights down SR. Lights up SL on the dining
room. KILLIAN and ANGIE are huddled
together hiding under the dining room table.
ANGIE becomes conscious of their intimacy.*

ANGIE

Get off me!

KILLIAN

Girl, you grabbed me!

ANGIE

No I didn't. (*scooting out from under the table*) Just give me
a minute here. I need to think.

KILLIAN

You're not thinking about going back up there, are you?

ANGIE

I don't know.

KILLIAN

Seriously? I mean, I believe in ghosts as much as the next
guy, but I doubt that's what we're dealing with here. I know I
panicked back there a little bit... but that's not because I'm
afraid of ghosts. I'm afraid of crazy people!

ANGIE

Well, obviously Ronnie is crazy. We know that. But that
doesn't mean she's not here. You said it yourself, you believe
in ghosts. So how do we know some part of her isn't still
here in this house?

KILLIAN

Okay.

                              ANGIE
And I don't know about Ronnie or what he's going through
right now, but I have to admit, I felt something.

                              KILLIAN
What do you mean, like the ghost touched you?

                              ANGIE
No! Like… the room changed… the light and the air…
something happened in that moment. You didn't notice it?

                              KILLIAN
Can't say that I did.

                    Angie looks disappointed.

                              KILLIAN
But… there was a lot going on, so… that's not to say it
didn't happen.

                              ANGIE
All I'm saying is that if she is here… somehow… I want…
(*starts to cry*) I just want to… try to talk to her.

                    *ANGIE sobs and KILLIAN awkwardly tries to
                    comfort her.*

                              KILLIAN
So what do you want to do?

                              ANGIE
(*trying to compose herself*) I want to go back up there.
Just… give me a second...

                              KILLIAN
Take all the time you need.

*ANGIE takes a few deep breaths. Lights fade on
KILLIAN and ANGIE and fade up on the
bedroom.*

*The room has taken on a different light. DANI is
moving around, clearly agitated and searching
for something, paging through dusty old books.*

RONNIE

Dani?

She doesn't respond.

RONNIE
I can see you. Can you see me?

*DANI'S frustration mounts. She says nothing,
but slowly locks her eyes on RONNIE. It's hard
to tell whether she's looking at him or through
him. He remains a safe distance away.*

RONNIE
Dani, please talk to me. Tell me why we're here. Did you
want us to come? Because I felt like you called us here
tonight.

*DANI sits on the end of the bed, trying to collect
her thoughts. Unable to concentrate, she begins
to cry.*

RONNIE
Oh no. What's wrong? Dani, please. Why are you crying? I
see you. I'm right here with you now. You're not alone
anymore.

DANI looks up as if she hears something.

RONNIE
Oh my God. Did you hear me? Can you hear me?

> *But it's clear that DANI is responding to some
> other sound. She goes to the bedroom door,
> opens it, lights up on the dining room and
> staircase.*

DANI
(*Shouting downstairs angrily*) I'm coming!

> *ANGIE screams. She and KILLIAN, who were
> just about to start up the stairs, run into the
> dining room and back under the table. Lights
> down on the dining room and bedroom, lights up
> on the front door.*

TRICIA
What was that? Did you hear that?

KEVIN
Of course we heard it. It was a blood curdling scream.

TRICIA
I'm sorry I don't know who can hear what anymore! We
should leave here and call 911!

KEVIN
No!

TRICIA
Are you serious?

KEVIN

We'll all get in trouble!

TRICIA

In trouble? We could all get killed here.

MEGAN

I agree with Tricia. Something really dark is happening in
that house.

SUZANNE

(*finally more composed*) Dark? What do you mean?

MEGAN

I'm just saying... like... Ronnie's weird energy... and this
house. I mean, it's creepy how it's just been sitting here
rotting, empty for so long.

KEVIN

Why didn't anyone ever buy this house?

TRICIA

Because her parents never put it on the market.

MEGAN

Why is that though?

TRICIA

I have no idea.

KEVIN

So it's just gonna sit here for eternity... exactly the way they
left it? Sounds to me like the perfect place for a ghost.

MEGAN

Maybe the place is...

SUZANNE

What? Haunted?

MEGAN

Well, this isn't the first time someone claims to have seen strange things here.

TRICIA

Megan, don't.

KEVIN

What?

MEGAN

We've all heard stories over the years about kids who say they've seen a girl in the upstairs window.

TRICIA

This is not helpful, Megan.

MEGAN

Well, it's true. There's the story about the girl in the window, and I've heard that the neighbors complain about noises coming from the house at night.

KEVIN

Oh, I think this house *is* haunted. And so what if it is? If you think about it, isn't a ghost just a person who died?

TRICIA

You can't be serious.

KEVIN

I am. Like, wasn't that your friend? And... I think about my mom... who's really sick. And I don't want her to die...

MEGAN

Oh my God, Kevin… we didn't know that… of course not.

KEVIN

But she is going to.

MEGAN

I'm so sorry.

KEVIN

And when she does… I want to believe that she can come back. As a ghost… or whatever.

MEGAN

Sure… that makes sense.

KEVIN

And I'll be open to it. Like… Cuz it's my mom. Her soul or spirit or whatever. So I won't be afraid.

SUZANNE

Well if this house is haunted, we *know* that ghost.

TRICIA

Shut up, Suzanne. There is no ghost.

SUZANNE

You shut up, Tricia! Stop acting like you have all the answers and everyone is crazy but you. You're a pathetic liar. You know it, I know it, and Dani knows it. That's why she's back! You're just as responsible as I am for what happened.

TRICIA

What?!?

SUZANNE

You pitted us against each other. Dani and me. All the time. We weren't competitive. You just made it seem like everything between us was a contest to try to drive a wedge between us.

TRICIA

That is such a lie.

MEGAN

No it isn't.

TRICIA

Excuse me? Megan, you cannot be serious right now.

MEGAN

Well... I... I just think Suzanne has a point. I recall quite a few times when it felt like... like you were intentionally causing conflict between them.

TRICIA

What is wrong with you people? You think Dani is haunting us because of some middle school social drama? That is stupid! Why am I still standing here? Bye, losers.

SUZANNE

Yeah, just walk away and act like you had nothing to do with what happened to her.

TRICIA

Suzanne, you're the one who said it was *your* fault. So what did *you* do to her?

SUZANNE

It wasn't what I did. It was just... It was my adderall that killed her.

MEGAN

What? Why did you have adderall?

SUZANNE

Because I have ADHD. I've been taking it since 5th grade.

MEGAN

I didn't know that, Suzanne.

SUZANNE

No, none of you did. Not even Dani. No one knew except Tricia. (*to Tricia*) You were the only one who knew that I had that medication. But what I never could figure out is why you would take my pills and give them to Dani?

> *Lights down on the front door, lights up on the dining room. ANGIE and KILLIAN are under the table again.*

KILLIAN

Holy Moses! Jesus God in Heaven! We're gonna die!

ANGIE

Be quiet!

KILLIAN

Oh God. Oh my God. We have to get out of here.

ANGIE

Killian, you heard that?

KILLIAN

(*also terrified*) Yes, I heard it.

ANGIE

You heard her voice?

KILLIAN

Yes! Well, I heard *a* voice.

ANGIE

And what did the voice say?

KILLIAN

It said, "I'm coming."

ANGIE

What is happening, Killian? Oh my God.

KILLIAN

Is that what you heard?

ANGIE

Yes, that's what I heard!

KILLIAN

Maybe it was Ronnie.

ANGIE

That did not sound like Ronnie.

KILLIAN

It didn't even sound human.

ANGIE

What is happening?

KILLIAN

We're going to die here tonight, Angie. So I'm thinking…
you should probably know… I'm in love with you -

ANGIE

Oh no.

KILLIAN

I've had a crush on you since 6th grade.

ANGIE

Killian, please -

KILLIAN

And if this is our last night on Earth maybe we should -

ANGIE

Shut it, okay? Just… shut your mouth! We are not going to die!

KILLIAN

I don't know. It's looking pretty likely.

ANGIE

We're going to get out of here. I thought you said you weren't afraid of ghosts.

KILLIAN

Well, yeah, in theory, but I've never actually been in the presence of one before. So I guess I just didn't know how truly terrifying it would be!

ANGIE

Ronnie is still up there.

KILLIAN

Oh well! I'm not going back up there.

> *The floorboards creak as Dani descends the staircase.*

ANGIE

Killian?

KILLIAN

Oh no.

ANGIE

She's coming down to us.

KILLIAN

We are going to die.

> *Lights down on the dining room, lights up*
> *outside at the front door.*

KEVIN

Guys, there's a lot of weird noises coming from in there. Should we go back in? They might need our help.

TRICIA

No way!

SUZANNE

You're so selfish.

TRICIA

Are you going back in there, Suzanne?

> *SUZANNE tries to will herself to do it.*

TRICIA

That's right. And your brother is in there! But somehow I'm the selfish-

SUZANNE

SHUT UP! I hate you so much. You told Dani about the adderall. I know you stole it from me! It's your fault she's dead.

MEGAN

Both of you, stop it!

TRICIA

I never told her about it! NEVER! And I certainly never took your stupid pills!

SUZANNE

You're lying!

KEVIN

Guys, please! They need our help!

TRICIA

I only mentioned it once…

SUZANNE

Oh my God, I knew it.

TRICIA

And it wasn't to Dani!

SUZANNE

Then how would she have known? I don't believe you.

TRICIA

Fine, don't believe me. But I'm telling you the truth.

MEGAN

You told Angie.

SUZANNE

Is that…? Did you…?

TRICIA

Yes. I only mentioned it to Angie because you kept bragging about your A plus PLUS on your term paper when the rest of us barely eked out a B and Dani got a D! I mean, imagine how that made her feel. Angie and I were fed up with you rubbing it in our faces so I just said... It was probably easier for you because you were on meds. The rest of us were struggling to get it done and you just powered through it with some... superhuman focus.

MEGAN

Wow.

KEVIN

Yeah. Wow. You are all very troubled.

TRICIA

Oh shut up! You know nothing about any of us.

KEVIN

And at this point, I don't want to know anything else! My grandma warned me about hanging out with Killian. Now here I am wrapped up in this murder mystery -

MEGAN

Hey! She wasn't murdered!

KEVIN

Well it seems to me like no one really knows for sure what happened. Maybe she was murdered. Or maybe she's just so pissed you're all hating on each other, making all these accusations about what happened, that her ghost has come back to set the record straight.

MEGAN

Please stop, Kevin. There is nothing to set straight.

KEVIN

Killian said the neighbors heard her fighting with her parents that night, maybe they had something to do with it.

MEGAN

That did not happen! Her parents were good people. Even if somebody gave her that adderall, nobody knew she had a freaking heart problem!

SUZANNE

(*heading toward the door*) I'm going back in.

TRICIA

Don't, Suzanne! (*trying to block her*)

SUZANNE

Get out of my way! Don't try to act like you care what happens to me at this point!

TRICIA

But I do! I do care about you, Suzanne. I care about all of you, and I don't want anyone to get hurt. (*getting emotional*) I'm sorry.

MEGAN

(*consoling her*) Tricia.

TRICIA

I'm sorry, Megan. I don't know what's wrong with me. I never wanted to hurt you. To hurt any of you. And Dani... (*sobbing*) I never... Please, you have to believe me.

SUZANNE

Fine. We believe you. Just... MOVE!

> *Lights up on the dining room. DANI is pacing*
> *the room while ANGIE and KILLIAN hide under*

*the table. She's frustrated, restless. RONNIE
stands on the staircase watching. A few seconds
later, SUZANNE enters through the front door.
It's clear she now sees DANI too. RONNIE looks
at her and puts his finger to his mouth to quiet
her. They are all rapt. DANI pulls out a chair
and sits down at the table. ANGIE and KILLIAN
cling to each other, petrified.*

DANI
(*as if speaking to her parents*) I told you I'm sorry. I just
don't get it. Maybe there's something wrong with me. Did
you ever consider that? (*Beat*) You can punish me all you
want! Take my phone away! Ground me! It won't matter! I
can't do it!

*DANI pounds her hands on the table and ANGIE
screams.*

*KEVIN, TRICIA and MEGAN outside
continuous.*

KEVIN
It sounds like they're fighting.

MEGAN
Who is fighting with who?

KEVIN
We have to go back in there.

TRICIA
No!

*A light switches on from offstage and a dog
starts barking.*

KEVIN

Oh no! It's the neighbors!

TRICIA

Can they actually hear… ?

KEVIN

(*opening the front door*) Come on!

MEGAN

(*following him, then to Tricia who is still in tears*) We have
to, Tricia, or they're going to see us and call the cops!

> *Lights out on the area outside the front door.*
> *MEGAN, TRICIA, and KEVIN are inside now,*
> *frozen in the entryway. It's clear from their*
> *reactions that they all see and hear DANI too.*

DANI

I can't do anything right anymore. Nothing is good enough
for you! It's not that I'm not trying. I just don't get it. And I
fail. I'm a failure at life. (*She moves toward the stairs,
causing Ronnie to plaster himself to the wall to make room.*)
I hate school! I hate my life! (*From the top of the steps*) I
hate you!

> *DANI goes into the bedroom and slams the door.*
> *They all freeze. KILLIAN and ANGIE slowly*
> *move out from under the table. SUZANNE sees*
> *ANGIE and flies into a rage.*

SUZANNE

(*to Angie*) It's your fault!

MEGAN

Suzanne!

SUZANNE

The pills! You stole my pills.

Angie looks at Tricia.

TRICIA

(*to Angie*) It had to be you. You were the only one who knew she had them.

ANGIE

What? Why would you…?

SUZANNE

You stopped by my house after school that day, Angie. You said you needed to use our bathroom.

TRICIA

Angie, why would you do that?

ANGIE

I didn't…

SUZANNE

You absolutely did. (*crying*) Why? Why, Angie?

ANGIE

(*crying*) Because… she said… she couldn't concentrate.

RONNIE

Angie!

ANGIE

I'm sorry. I'm… so… so… sorry…

RONNIE

You killed her.

KILLIAN

STOP IT!

RONNIE

You did!

TRICIA

If you hadn't given her those pills, Dani would still be alive.

KILLIAN

Guys, don't! She said it herself, Ang. It's not your fault. Isn't that what she said, Ronnie?

SUZANNE

It absolutely IS her fault. You stole from me, Angie! You gave her those pills and they killed her!

ANGIE

It's all my fault. I'm sorry. I'm so…

KILLIAN

You didn't know what would happen! It was her heart!

SUZANNE

You don't give medication to someone without a doctor's prescription.

KILLIAN

Oh please, Suzanne! I've taken your adderall before! So have half my friends.

SUZANNE

What is wrong with you?

KILLIAN

It didn't kill me! But what if I had, Suzanne? You left your pills out. So if something happened to me, would it have been your fault?

SUZANNE

What? No!

KILLIAN

It's not your fault, Angie. You couldn't have known what would happen.

MEGAN

Her parents didn't even know, Angie.

KILLIAN

It was her choice to take those pills. *Her* choice! Accidents happen. None of you meant to hurt her. What is the point in blaming each other? It won't bring her back!

There is a tense silence. Then…

DANI (*from upstairs*)

Hello? (*pause*) Yeah. I can't really talk now. I'm… I'm trying to study.

KEVIN

What is she doing?

DANI

Please. I can't get into a big discussion about this now.

RONNIE

I think… She's reliving that night.

KILLIAN
So… all of this at the table…

KEVIN
That was the fight with her parents.

SUZANNE
Is she talking to someone up there now? Was someone else in her room that night?

They all look at each other suspiciously.

MEGAN
No. She's talking… on the phone…

RONNIE slowly follows her up the stairs. Lights go up in the bedroom. DANI paces, listening to someone as if they are on the phone on speaker. The others follow RONNIE into the room as the one-sided conversation continues. We hear DANI'S reactions, but never hear who she's talking to.

DANI
(*distressed*) Nobody is hiding anything. Why do you have to make this such a big deal?

TRICIA
(*whispering to Ronnie*) Who do you think she's talking to?

RONNIE
Shhh.

DANI

Honestly, you're reading into it - (*The person on the other end of the conversation has clearly cut her off, she reacts with impatience*). We don't *always* have to do everything together! Sometimes it can just be.. two of us.

SUZANNE

Which two of us?

TRICIA

Probably her and Angie.

DANI

Veronica is my friend! She's OUR friend. That's all.

RONNIE

Oh God.

There's a pause while the person on the other end responds.

DANI

Please, stop. I told you, I have to study. (*the person continues and Dani's impatience peaks*) Why are you doing this right now, Megan?

The others turn to see MEGAN in tears.

MEGAN

Because I know Veronica is in love with you.

DANI

That's just... that's not true.

MEGAN

It is true! She admitted it to me.

DANI

Well... so what then! Please, Megan, just leave it alone.

MEGAN

Like you two are always leaving me alone?

DANI

No we are not.

MEGAN

You are! You're excluding me. It's always the two of you now. And you know the others aren't as close with me. I mean, Suzanne has Tricia and Tricia has Angie. But I really only ever had you and Veronica.

DANI

I'm sorry, Megan. We don't mean to -

MEGAN

You're being a really bad friend, Dani.

DANI

I'm sorry... *(beat)* Listen, I really have to study. If I fail my biology exam, I will fail the class for the year. So... just... please. Can we talk later? I have to go.

MEGAN

(losing her composure) Fine! Forget it! You and Veronica can just go on with your secret love affair and leave me out of it! I don't need you! I don't need any of you!

> *It's clear from DANI'S reaction that MEGAN abruptly hangs up on her. As DANI paces the room upset by the call, the others stare at MEGAN in confusion.*

RONNIE

What did you do?

MEGAN

It was true. All of it.

RONNIE

So what if it was?

MEGAN

I was only saying… you… you dicn't have to do that to me!
I hated that you were together because… I was so alone.

RONNIE

You were alone?

MEGAN

Yes! And I was angry.

> *As the following argument ensues, DANI paces
> behind them recklessly, then abruptly turns
> upstage. Something is wrong. She holds her
> chest.*

RONNIE

My God. You made her feel guilty!

MEGAN

I'm sorry.

RONNIE

What, were you judging us?

MEGAN

I didn't mean to -

TRICIA

Why would you do that, Megan?

SUZANNE

(*Trying to calm Ronnie*) We all knew it, Ronnie, and it was fine.

TRICIA

We didn't care.

ANGIE

You didn't have to do that to her!

MEGAN

Well you didn't have to give her the pills that killed her, Angie!

ANGIE

She asked for my help. She needed help.

> *DANI'S eyes are wide, and she looks as if she's in shock. She continues to hold her chest, struggling to breathe.*

SUZANNE

You and Dani shouldn't have known about those pills in the first place. That's on you, Tricia!

TRICIA

If you didn't want anybody to know you were on meds then why did you tell me? You shouldn't have said anything about it if it was such a big secret!

KEVIN

(*noting that Dani is struggling*) Guys, stop!

RONNIE

(*To Megan*) You made her feel ashamed! There was no shame in her loving me.

MEGAN

I didn't know for sure how she felt I was just being honest about how *I f*elt.

RONNIE

No one cares how you felt! I loved her and she loved me, and that had nothing to do with you!

MEGAN

And so what? You *loved* each other, so you both just stopped caring about the rest of your friends? About me?

RONNIE

What a tragedy. You didn't have anybody to hang out with for a few days.

> *The others take notice as DANI continues to*
> *struggle. They are frozen, terrified; all but*
> *RONNIE and MEGAN who continue to argue.*

TRICIA

What is happening?

MEGAN

It was more than a few days. It was weeks. I know that for almost a month you were sneaking into her room at night.

RONNIE

What?

MEGAN

You were spending every moment together. And I knew you would be there that night.

RONNIE

But… (*confused*) I wasn't. I wasn't there…

DANI collapses on the bed and takes what appears to have been her last breath.

MEGAN

I know it was you!

RONNIE

No! There's no way! I didn't - No!

ANGIE

Dani!

RONNIE

I couldn't have been there.

MEGAN

Maybe not at that exact moment, but you had to be the one in her room that night. I know you were sneaking out every night around that time so you could be together.

RONNIE

How do you know that?

MEGAN

Because I followed you. I saw you.

RONNIE

You were spying on us?

ANGIE

(*reacting to Dani's collapse*) Ronnie?

MEGAN

Yes! I saw you… you'd move the picnic table and climb through her window.

RONNIE is in front of the broken window. DANI is, as she was that night, lifeless on the bed.

RONNIE

(*remembering*) I… I did. I'd come through the window.

The lights shift. RONNIE relives that night. He quietly pretends to close the window, then turns to see her on the bed. At first, he smiles, thinking she's fallen asleep. He moves some books off the bed, sits down beside her and kisses her forehead. Then he notices how cold she is. He puts his hand to her mouth and realizes she's not breathing. He can barely breathe himself. He backs up, clumsily, in a state of shock, and smashes what's left of the window pane with his elbow.

KILLIAN

The window.

RONNIE lets out an almost inaudible cry and falls to his knees.

KEVIN

The thud.

RONNIE panics imagining he can hear her father yell up the stairs; he pulls himself up and scrambles back toward the window as if to go out the way he came in. He tries to open the window, but all these years later, it's impossible.

RONNIE looks back at them. There is a pause in the action as they all come to grips with the truth.

The lights shift again. DANI slowly rises from the bed then walks to the door. But before she exits, she turns around one last time.

DANI

(*to all*) It's not your fault.

DANI exits. The girls gather around RONNIE. They hold him and cry together. KEVIN and KILLIAN exchange glances, as if neither could have imagined the night would turn out like this. After a few beats the neighbor's light switches on and the dog starts barking again.

KILLIAN

(*drawing their attention to the neighbor's light*) Guys, I think we gotta get outta here.

KEVIN

Yeah.

There's an awkward silence as they look at each other, unsure.

ANGIE

So, I guess we'll just see each other tomorrow then… at school.

RONNIE

I guess so.

ANGIE

I'll look for you guys. Ronnie, we have lunch together, right?

RONNIE

We do.

ANGIE

Okay. So I'll see you at lunch.

RONNIE

Okay. That… sounds good.

ANGIE

And uh… Megan, you have our same lunch period, don't
you?

MEGAN

Yes, I do.

ANGIE

Cool.

RONNIE

Maybe we can all sit together.

MEGAN

Really? (*choking up*) I would love that.

ANGIE

Yeah. So… let's plan to do that then.

RONNIE

Cool.

MEGAN

Cool.

SUZANNE
I'm so sorry, Ronnie. I'm here for you... you know... if you
need -

TRICIA
We all are.

RONNIE
Thanks. I'm sorry I made you come out here.

SUZANNE
I'm actually glad you brought us out here tonight.

RONNIE
No, it was stupid, I shouldn't have...

SUZANNE
No, you needed to. Somehow you knew she needed us. We
were all supposed to be here tonight.

RONNIE
Yeah. I guess I did. Thanks, Suzanne.

SUZANNE
Sure. (*shifting into big sister mode*) Killian, let's go. You're
walking with me.

> *They all descend the stairs and make their way
> outside as they deliver these final lines.*

KILLIAN
Tricia, you should walk home with us since you're going in
the same direction.

TRICIA
No, it's fine... you guys go ahead.

KILLIAN

What? No.

SUZANNE

Come on, Tricia. You can't walk by yourself in the middle of the night.

TRICIA

Okay. If you're sure you wouldn't mind.

SUZANNE

I'm sure.

Beat.

KEVIN

So… yeah. Well, it was nice meeting you all. We should do this again sometime.

The others react to this.

KILLIAN

Kevin, you walk with Ronnie. He lives near your Grammy's house.

KEVIN

Okay.

ANGIE

Megan, we should walk together too.

KILLIAN

Yeah. Nobody should be walking home alone.

SUZANNE

Wow. Now he's Mr. Responsible.

                    ANGIE
Killian. Give me your phone.

                    KILLIAN
(*handing her the phone*) Okay.

          *ANGIE types her number into his phone then
          hands it back to him.*

                    ANGIE
Call me.

          *KILLIAN nods calmly, then as ANGIE and
          MEGAN exit, he celebrates. SUZANNE pulls
          him off in the other direction with TRICIA
          following. RONNIE looks up at the house.*

                    KEVIN
You ready to go, Ronnie?

                    RONNIE
Yeah. I'm ready now.

          *KEVIN AND RONNIE exit as the lights go
          down.*

                    END OF PLAY